JUSTIN MAXIMILIAN

SECURITY GUARD EXTRAORDINAIRE

WRITTEN BY

Kate E. Sebastian

First Edition

July 2012

ISBN-10: 061566038X

ISBN-13: 978-0-615-66038-7

DEDICATION

To my husband who has kept me safe,

sound, and secure all these years.

ACKNOWLEDGEMENTS

Justin Maximilian, Security Guard Extraordinaire, couldn't have been written if it hadn't been for all the love, support, and encouragement extended to me by my friends and family, Pat, Mark, JoAnn, Paula, Joan, George, Rebecca, Brian, Stacy, Mike, David, and Sydney.

Another big round of thanks to all my writer critique friends, Karin, Nancy, Steve, Jean, Erik, Jim, Rena, Allen, Margaret, Lisa, Rachel, Emily, Jane, Shirley, Barbara, and Sarah, and to my writing coaches at College of DuPage, Nicolet College, University of Wisconsin, and the School of Arts in Rhinelander.

TABLE of CONTENTS

JUSTIN MAXIMILIAN
SECURITY GUARD EXTRAORDINAIRE

EGADS!

Being someone who appreciates and thrives on predictable outcomes, as illustrated by my habit of reading a book's last chapter first, I was about to discover real-life surprises can sometimes be a good thing. Who could have imagined one night of hanging out and engaging in innocent, seemingly incoherent banter at a small rundown barroom in Malto, Ohio, could have such a pivotal effect on a guy's life? Not me, Justin Maximilian, Security Guard Extraordinaire.

Unfortunately, the thread-bare remnants of my nearly non-existent social life continued to be severely restricted due to my horrendously erratic and inconvenient work hours as a security guard hired to serve and protect Oxford Shopping Mall. And so, after an overstaffing computer glitch provided me with an unexpected Friday night off, I quickly called my former high school buddy, Bill Taylor, to suggest we meet for a beer at Egads Corner Bar.

"Sure," Bill said, "I'll be right there."

Bill must have taken off running because he beat me there, even though I live in the aging brick apartment building just across the street. I arrived to find an icy-cold glass mug, dripping with beads of condensation, sitting on the bar and beckoning me with an inch of foam on top. I pulled out a padded red bar stool whose non-skid legs resisted my initial attempt and squeezed my tall, lanky self into the small empty space next to Bill. Huddled together at the far end of the bar rapidly becoming crowded with more happy hour patrons, I started getting the conversation rolling by asking, "How's Sue?"

"Don't ask," he said with a grump.

"What's wrong?" I asked, knowing he'd continue if prompted.

2

"Well," Bill started right in again, "she complains I never do anything around the house so I decided to surprise her by re-doing the pantry. I ripped out all the old wood shelves and installed new plastic-coated wire racks. And wouldn't you know it, she came home madder than hell."

As someone who doesn't have an iota of handyman skills and doesn't know the difference between a needle-nose pliers and a Phillips head screwdriver, I was mightily impressed with Bill's most recent building project—even if Sue wasn't.

"Why's that?" I asked.

"Just because I had the ingenuity to build tall shelves for the tall cans, and short shelves for the short cans, that's why. It seems that logic was lost on her. She was devastated the tall cans of beans couldn't share the same shelf space with all the other vegetables. Like they care."

"So how did you work it out?" I asked.

3

"We didn't. After your call, I got the hell outta there."

"Hmmm," I mused. "You left her alone with those mismatched vegetables?"

"Yep," he said. "To give her some time to cool off. And I'm hoping you feel up to sharing a pizza 'cause I'm not planning on eating at home tonight."

After twenty minutes of trying, I was able to hail down the bartender to order their Friday Night Super Special, an extra-large, he-man's meat-lover frozen pizza with extra cheese. As a single, working guy, pizza was standard fare for me. Bill considered it a special treat since Sue had a long-running passion for eating in Thai restaurants.

After swiping the side of his mouth smeared in marinara sauce onto his brown recycled paper napkin, Bill looked up and inquired as to my love life.

"Non-existent," I shrugged.

"No, really, Justin," he said. "Aren't there some nice, pretty broads over at your apartment complex just itching to go out with you?"

Attempting to avoid a direct answer, I glanced around the room. With everyone talking at the same time, I wondered if anyone was available for listening. Not that it mattered since the escalating din was getting close to the same noise level of Oxford Shopping Mall's emergency power back-up generators running at full throttle.

Making his way across the bar and causing the floor boards to vibrate beneath my feet, a scruffy gray-haired biker dude dressed in black leather grunted as he selected a chair at a table facing my direction. He may have been well past his prime to be considered cool, but as I value my life and all my limbs, I wasn't about to be the one to tell him. Other weekend warrior groupies sat down next to him—except the big-busted, black-haired mama who I suspect was

5

the leader's girlfriend. She stood in front of the juke box contemplating a music selection.

Still struggling to suppress my response to Bill's inquiry, I thought about the women available at Provincial Gardens. Cold shivers shot up my spine, forcing me to laugh out loud.

"Well, I think Brenda is still single," I blurted. "Maybe I should ask her out?"

"O.k., I'll bite. What's wrong with Brenda?"

"I've thought of giving her the nickname 'Thunder Thighs.' She isn't bad to look at, but she is so wide from side to side that if she was a trailer on the road, she'd need a spotter both in front and behind."

"Aw, come on!" Bill said. "She can't be that bad."

After downing three tall mugs of Big Bad Brewsters on tap, of course I was exaggerating and felt justified being cynical. And why not! From her apartment above mine, Brenda sounds like an elephant with an attitude tromping up and down. What was she doing? Crushing grapes to make wine? If I didn't know any better, I'd think Brenda was deliberately trying to irritate the heck out of me . . . or, hmmm, maybe she was trying to get my attention?

"So tell me," I asked Bill as I persisted with my grudge against Brenda by taking advantage of her absence and inability to defend herself. "Why is it that women built like Brenda have no trouble finding guys to go out with? She's got at least three or four guys mooning over her; guys with bigger biceps than me, guys who still have a full head of hair."

Bill swallowed his next bite of pizza, cleared his throat, and like he was an authority on the subject, he said distinctly, "It's because we don't feel threatened by women like Brenda. She would never get in a tither if a guy rebuilt her God-damned pantry shelves differently than she had expected. You see?"

I had a visual image of Bill's wife with her long, blonde hair and tall, shapely legs. Apparently, he hadn't been concerned about such threats when deciding to marry Sue.

Bill set down his empty beer mug on the bar, sighed, and said, "Well, I should get going."

"Say what? The night's still young!"

"I know, but I've got to go home and make up with Sue. Why don't we get together again next week?"

I started muttering something like, 'same time, same place,' when members of our inebriated bar crowd began cheering and clapping. We looked up to see a pretty, youngish woman provocatively dressed in a scanty red dress engaging in an impromptu private-turned-public lap dance for the benefit of the scruffy biker dude.

I quickly looked to the black-haired woman to see how she was taking it, but her face seemed void of emotion. Unlike her, the crowd went crazy.

"Yah! Oh Yah!"

"That 'a way!"

"Whoot Hoo! Whoot Hoo!"

Bill and I glanced at each other and laughed.

Then, as the woman in the red dress slowly circled around to face in our direction, we found ourselves staring at none other than Sue herself. When she knew she had his attention, Sue smiled and winked seductively at Bill.

The self-centered loudmouths in the bar grew quiet and we all watched Sue as she threw her right hand onto her hip and slowly high-stepped her way over to Bill. "Hey, big guy," she said, "whatt'a ya say we split this place?"

Bill stuttered something inaudible, grabbed his wallet off the bar, and hurried to follow Sue out the door.

About to lose their impromptu evening entertainment, the barroom patrons began expressing their disappointment by booing and flipping the bird. Before things got out of control with fists swinging in my direction, I decided to call it a night myself and left post haste. Thank goodness a middle-aged loser stumbling out the door didn't provoke them any further.

MOVING UP

I stepped outside Egads to be temporarily blinded by the setting sun. Immediately confronted with a blast of commuter bus exhaust followed by hot, muggy thermal air currents slapping me scentless, I diverted my attention to a commotion in front of my apartment building across the street. Two squad cars with revolving strobe lights held vigil by the front entrance and a crowd of spectators started assembling on the sidewalk. A rough-tough-and-ready police officer stood surveying the rooftop above the third floor windows.

Expecting to see hot and fiery flames devouring the building, I looked too.

"Holy shit," I said out loud. I didn't notice anything out of the ordinary, but still felt compelled to utter an expletive.

11

Assuming the worst, I took my time crossing the street. Bad news is bad news no matter when or how you get it. I preferred the delayed version myself. When I finally finished sauntering across the street, I was nabbed by our astute property manager, Lakshan Das, a third-generation Indian import who we lovingly dubbed, "Louie."

"Justin! Justin!" he hollered like I was hard of hearing. "Hey, Justin, you're a security guard, right?" he asked, as if he didn't know. "How'd you like to find the guys who did this?"

"Did what?"

"A couple of guys dressed in tan work uniforms set up a forty-foot extension ladder and they climbed through an open third-floor window to Jacobson's apartment. Right there in broad daylight they carried furniture, electronic equipment, and even his bedroom slippers down the stairs and into a moving van parked in front of the building. They cleaned him out, lock, stock, and barrel. They were well on their way before anyone realized what was going on."

"Pretty slick," I said, admiring their cunning and resourcefulness.

"Yeah, too slick. You willing to take the job?"

Admittedly, my security guard uniform gives me an outward appearance of someone important, someone in charge. But it was all a ruse.

Heck, I didn't even own a gun, yet alone carry one with me on the job. Giving the impression I had arrest powers, my bogus presence was surmised to thwart and/or intercede bad guys. In two years time, I had as yet to encounter a single one so apparently this premise works.

Apprehending and capturing crafty, world-class thieves would be stretching the concept a little thin; but I didn't want to disappoint Louie so I said yes, I'd try. Louie smiling and vigorously shaking my hand up and down like it was the rusty handle to the water pump in Cell Tower Park was thanks enough.

I hoped I wouldn't let him down.

After an evening with so much excitement, I went home to sleep. At four o'clock in the morning I had a gig at Munson Tire Factory. It wasn't too likely a band of snow tire thugs would be out and about at that time of day, but pity them if they were because they'd have to contend with my early morning orneriness and my lethal sixteen-inch flashlight.

At midnight, my slumber was interrupted when Brenda arrived at her apartment upstairs. A few minutes later, through the non-insulated, paper-thin walls of my apartment I heard her date leave on his juiced-up motor cycle with mufflers roaring, tempting a municipal fine had someone called it in. It wouldn't be me. I'm not the type to get involved in domestic issues, especially in the wee hours of the night.

Fortunate for me, I heard Brenda get ready for bed shortly thereafter, and we both settled down to a quiet night of sobering solitude.

The next week I was occupied with a series of late night security guard assignments. Not that I was reneging my commitment to catch Louie's thief. On the contrary, as soon as I found the time and energy I'd start some serious investigative moves, like placing a call down to the local precinct to see if they had come up with any leads. The only catch is the guys in blue don't have any reason to give me, a lowly security guard, any recognition or respect. And I don't blame them one bit; it goes with the territory.

On Thursday afternoon while zonked out on the couch, I heard a loud racket coming from Brenda's apartment right above mine. It sounded like furniture being hurled into a wall and glass shattering. Then I heard Brenda scream like a high-pitched jaguar about to leap on her prey.

I thrust my feet into my pant legs, yanked my jeans up to my waist, and lunged for the door. I stalled for a split second when I eyed my work shoes sitting by the front closet. I had extremely sensitive feet and hated like heck going anywhere without them, but Brenda's screaming prompted me into action. I flew up the staircase barefooted.

Rushing to the rescue with a set of master keys in hand was Louie. His hands were shaking something awful and when he saw me, he relinquished the keys to me. Without hesitating, I turned the lock and roughly shoved the door wide open. As we heard the doorknob smashing into the interior wall, we looked inside. Other than the apartment being in a big upheaval, I couldn't detect anything wrong. Brenda was sitting on the floor dressed in light pink workout clothes and a pink ribbon pinning back her long brown hair. She appeared relieved to see me.

"What's wrong?" I asked in a state of panic.

"The, th--, the, burglar," she stuttered.

"The burglar was here?" Louie and I exclaimed simultaneously.

"Yes!"

"Which way did he go?" I asked. Professionally trained in the art of observation, I nervously shifted my vision back and forth across the room as my hand instinctively reached for my trusty flashlight. Darn! I left it downstairs!

The hairs on the back of my neck stood erect in anticipation as I scanned the room one more time. Where was the burglar hiding? Did he go back down the ladder protruding through Brenda's open living room window?

"He's here!" Brenda screamed at me. "He's right here!"

She wiggled herself to a standing position. Lying on the floor I saw a somewhat stunned and slightly squished young punk lying prone against

17

the hardwood flooring. I gritted my teeth as I realized I had just overlooked the obvious, a fact that wouldn't look so good if included on my resume. But I was impressed that Brenda, an inexperienced civilian, had captured the culprit single-handedly.

What a woman!

I silently retracted the comment I made about her a few days earlier.

Then I kicked into high gear. Before the ninety-five pounder could get up and cause me trouble, I reached into my back pocket to retrieve a handy set of plastic hand-cuffs, strapped them around his sorry wrists, and then I reached to help him stand up. Well, well, I thought. At least he was old enough to sport a mustache.

"The police are on their way!" Louie shouted.

"Good work, Louie," I complimented him.

A brigade of officers and lab techs ascended on the crime scene. Brenda and I hugged the living room wall, trying not to be a nuisance. I sighed a sense of relief when the offender was finally ushered out the front door. Dealing with thugs on a face-to-face basis sent my skinny, bow-legged knees to knocking. Not an admirable trait for a tough-guy security guard like me.

"You're bleeding!" Brenda exclaimed with a sincere look of concern for my well-being.

"I am?"

In the confusion, I had stepped on broken glass with my tender bare feet. It was a miracle I hadn't noticed until now. Brenda ushered me to sit on a dining room chair whereupon she tended to my wounds, swiping my feet with tiny antiseptic sheets and applying water-proof sports bandages to the cuts.

"Well," Brenda said, "the going rate for rescuing me is a fine, home-cooked meal."

"It is?"

Brenda twirled around and headed for her kitchen. Moments later, she returned donned with a pair of humungous oven mitts and set down a hot and bubbly casserole dish in front of me. Then I did what I imagine any other guy would do under similar circumstances. I grabbed onto a big serving spoon and dished up each one of us big chunks of chicken and vegetables smothered in a thick and creamy white sauce.

On the side, Brenda served hot, flaky biscuits smothered with little square pats of butter. She was some cook.

My interest in Brenda was piqued to a whole new level and once again I ostracized myself for my previous slanderous comment. While sitting across from each other over glasses of chilled white wine, I got up the nerve to talk to Brenda.

"Say," I said. "Would you like to join me and my friend for a beer at Egads tomorrow night?"

I gulped after hearing her response. Imagine her going out with me, a lowly security guard.

MALTO JUNK YARD

Happiness has never been so terrifying. During my first date with Brenda, my insides got all twisted and knotted up, my feet no longer touched the ground, and like a first-time novice shoplifter the palms of my hands got all hot and sweaty. Then I became light headed, had trouble concentrating, and figured I was a goner until the next time the congealed grease on the gear shafts of my brain dissolved like that on my car's transmission and I got the chance to wrap my arms tight as a fan belt around Brenda.

I hadn't needed to worry.

I soon discovered dating Brenda was like riding a Ferris wheel at top speed. One minute you were holding on tight and screaming as you twirled and felt like free falling over the edge. The next minute while headed back to the top, you felt euphoric like floating on air as though you were wearing angel wings.

23

One thing was for sure.

I never intended to let go of Brenda.

Everywhere she went, Brenda bragged about my exploits as a security guard, continually bolstering my self-confidence. With an ego inflated as big as a hot air balloon, I avoided straight pins, scissors, and the pointy end of sharp knives. Not that I had ever been a big fan of handling knives. Pity me if I ever became engaged in an all-out brawl with a hoodlum sporting a switchblade because I fainted at the tiniest sight of blood—mine or anyone else's.

I did have the awesome responsibility of serving and protecting the 9,462 Malto residents who came shopping at Oxford Shopping Mall every week, give or take an extra hundred out-of-town sightseers who came to watch the car crushing machine over at Malto Junk Yard. Ever since Bart Bartholomew went ballistic and created a blog on the World Wide Web, Malto Junk Yard became the eighth wonder of the world. Bart set up a seven-tier scaffolding of bleachers, offered refreshments like beer and pop corn, and even provided three sky-blue port-a-potties.

Brenda and I became Friday night regulars. My friend Bill Taylor joined us whenever he could get away, but he always came alone. It seems Sue didn't appreciate our new form of entertainment.

Late Tuesday afternoon, I got a surprise jingle-jingle, toot-toot on my Smartphone. It was from Bart. I was honored because Bart Bartholomew was the next best thing to a celebrity this side of Malto, Ohio.

"Hey, Justin," he began, "I hear you're the most popular security guard around."

"*Me*?"

"Yeah, I was calling to ask for your help. We've been having a rash of break-ins here at the junk yard, and I thought you'd be the right man to crack the case."

25

Good thing we weren't in person because my jaw was dragging across my kitchen floor. Apparently Brenda's rumors had just netted the biggest break of my career. And now the pressure was really on because if I were to screw up this mission, I'd be disappointing both of them.

"I could also throw in a couple of free tickets to the car crushing show," Bart added, upping the ante.

"What do you want me to do?" I asked.

I hated leaving Brenda stranded alone yet another night of the week to work at the junk yard, but I had an ulterior motive. I needed some extra cash to buy her something special for her birthday which was coming up in two weeks on the summer solstice, June 21st. The clock was ticking. I was running out of time.

When I arrived at the junk yard, I was in for one more surprise. Bart broke the news I'd be working with a partner. My eyes widened when I saw him. He was no ordinary guard dog. Besides having two ears, one tail, and four legs, it wasn't easy to recognize him as a part of the canine species. He stood inches away from me with his barred teeth dripping and oozing with saliva, half his right ear chewed off, and the muted brown hair on his back stood straight up like a buzz haircut.

I nervously shifted my peripheral vision to the tallest car on top of the junk pile, a four-door Studebaker Bullet Nose if I could see it correctly. But instead of running for the junk pile and making myself a moving target, I stood breathlessly in one spot. I might not be brave and courageous, but I wasn't stupid. Even if he tried to pee on my pant leg, I couldn't be persuaded to move from my small designated spot amongst heaps of rusty car parts. Instead, I stood my ground in a feeble attempt to proclaim myself as alpha. After all, Homo sapiens stood upright and he didn't.

"What kind is it?" I asked.

"He's a unique, one-of-a-kind breed," Bart boasted. "He's a Pitty Bull Pinscher."

"A whatttt?"

"Part Pit Bull, part Bull Mastiff, with a little Doberman Pinscher thrown in."

From the look of his front incisors and the intense glare of his eyes, I knew I didn't want to mess around with Bully Boy. And that's no bull either.

"Just one look at Bully Boy here should be enough to scare a prowler away, don't you think? Maybe you don't need a security guard after all."

"Ohhh, I still need a security guard," responded Bart, "to keep Bully Boy under control. People don't know he's a real sweetie pie of a lap dog. Once he started chasing a guy, that guy could drop dead of a heart attack. Then I could get slammed with a law suit by the guy's grieving widow or his ailing grandmother. Why,

I'd become penniless, homeless, and hopeless—a whole lot 'less' than I am now."

"Sweetie pie, my foot," I thought.

I wondered what was worth protecting here at the junk yard, but it wasn't up to me to judge my clients and what they considered valuable. After all, I'd fight tooth and nail to keep anyone from messing with my antique marble collection, which was the reason I kept it stored in the coal-black safe hidden deep inside the back of my closet. Agates, slags, cat's eyes, and especially tiger's eyes can be fairly valuable, not that mine were worth much more than a month of groceries. The bigger marbles, called shooters, were my personal favorites.

"But whatever you do," Bart continued, "make sure you lock up the storage shed tight because I can't risk both of them getting loose."

"Both of them?" I gulped. "You've got two Pitty Bull Pinschers?"

"Yeah, a man can't be too careful."

My first time moonlighting for Malto Junk Yard was set for Friday night, the biggest event Bart had scheduled so far.

As promised on the printed flyers spread across town, the half-time session of the Malto Car Crushing Show would feature smashing up and totally demolishing old Judge Werner's beat-up Edsel. The engine block was cracked, leather seats were torn to expose a matting of horse hair, and rusty outer rims were almost non-existent. But still, sentimental citizens of Malto considered it an injustice to treat their town's icon in such a vicious manner and they feverously began a campaign to get it restored and displayed at the historical museum on the corner of Main Street and Ristow Lane.

I found it endearing that Brenda went along with this small special interest group including people like Louie, our apartment manager, but I cringed when I learned Brenda was planning to participate in picketing the junk yard.

I was about to protest her protest when I looked into her soft, big brown eyes and I gave up that idea.

Well, maybe just this one time, I relented.

"Save the Edsel!"

"Bart, give up the Edsel!"

"We want the Edsel!"

Practical guys like me and Bart Bartholomew knew foregoing his sales price of $39.99 wasn't the issue here. In today's economic crisis, restoration costs would be enough to bankrupt the town and all the rest of us who were struggling to make ends meet. Unfortunately, the local do-gooders weren't as practical as us. To prove it, they took their campaign to an even higher level. They called in the big guns, the American Vintage Car Association.

Late in the afternoon I warmed up Bully Boy, Bart's Pitty Bull Pinscher, by walking him around the outer perimeter of the junk yard. As we passed Judge Werner's Edsel, I became freaked out when I took a look at it up close and personal. It had an odd-shaped grill centered on its front end that resembled a mouth gapping open in horror, exactly like Edvard Munch's painting, "The Scream."

Knowing the trouble brewing over the Edsel, I saw its howling grill as a sign we shouldn't be tampering with fate—we shouldn't be putting this rare vintage in the car crusher in front of a large group of angry protesters. But being a person who avoids conflict, I kept my mouth shut and didn't elect to share my narrow-minded opinion with anyone else.

I felt thankful I didn't get myself torn into shreds in the process of spending time with Bully Boy, but I began to worry even more about crowd control as I watched a countless number of people falling into line behind the entrance booth. Then I heard a loud commotion and looked to see Judge Werner himself as he started to take a seat in the first row of bleachers.

Still possessing his sense of public appeal, the Judge turned around, looked up to face the crowd, and gave a simply half wave. The crowd lovingly responded back with a round of hand clapping.

"Whoooot Whoooo!" a wolf whistle pierced the air. "Whoooot Whooo!"

With the crowd's mounting tension, Bully Boy began salivating white foam around his muzzle. I slowly but surely ushered my assigned guard dog back to his shed.

When I returned to the front yard, I scanned the bleachers until I saw Brenda sitting there with her long brown hair blowing in a gust of wind. I felt tiny bursts of pride until I saw Bill throw his arm around her and whisper something into her ear, sending alarms of jealousy pulsating in my veins. What was I doing down here? I should have been up in the bleachers with Brenda!

"And NOW for our feature presentation," shouted Bart from his megaphone. "It's time to crush Judge Werner's Edsel!"

A roar escaped from the crowd, punctuated by an unexpected spokesperson from the American Vintage Car Association who had a megaphone of her own.

"You can't do that! Edsels are classics!" she screeched.

"Go to hell," yelled someone from the crowd, followed by a tub of popcorn sailing through the air, resulting in an all-out melee.

The shouting escalated to a higher octave and things would have erupted into one big fist fight if it hadn't been for the ugly snarl behind me. I turned just in time to see a flash of brown fur racing into the throng of people, scattering the crowd in a thousand directions. Some people ran for the front gate, others scaled over the top of the six-foot tall privacy fence, and still others ran for the protection offered by skeletal old cars scattered throughout the junk yard.

"Oh, boy," I thought, "here we go."

Thinking I wouldn't be able to get Bully Boy under control by myself, I decided to do the next best thing. Save myself. And Brenda. I began scaling the bleachers to where I had last seen Brenda sitting with Bill's arm around her.

"Brenda! Brenda!" I yelled through the crowd. The sea of bleacher spectators was busy separating itself down the middle and there was Brenda sitting all by herself, with her hands patiently resting in her lap. I glanced around. Had Bill abandoned her in her time of need?

"Are you o.k.?" I asked breathlessly.

"Yeah," she said.

"Where's Bill?"

"I think he got stuck in the port-a-potty," Brenda laughed.

I looked at Brenda, back at the panicked crowd, and then the two of us sat there snickering and snorting as we saw the humor of it. People had packed themselves into Bart's tiny office and others had climbed up and were hanging onto the sides of the monstrosity of a crane. In the midst of the confusion we saw Bully Boy sitting in the dust with his tongue hanging out of his mouth. Humph, I thought, maybe he really is a sweetie pie?

A while later after most everyone left the car crushing event, Bart came up to me and congratulated me for saving the day by releasing Bully Boy. When I confessed I hadn't been the one to do anything, Bart mistakenly thought I was being too modest, and he attempted to congratulate me once again. That's when I saw a small figure still sitting in the front row of the bleachers. Yikes. Had Judge Werner fallen prey to a heart attack?

"Judge Werner," I said as I poked his arm, "Are you alright?"

"Yeah, yeah, what did you say?" he asked as I watched him reaching to adjust his hearing aid.

"ARE YOU ALRIGHT?" I repeated louder this time.

"I haven't had so much fun in a long time," laughed Judge Werner. "So when do you get around to crushing my Edsel?"

Just then the two of us heard Bart speak into his megaphone once more.

"And NOWWW, ladies and gentlemen, here's our feature presentation," he said.

Bart pushed the start button to the car crushing machine and we listened as the motor coughed, squeaked, shook and groaned. It shook and vibrated a few seconds more and then began its slow ascent towards the Edsel. We listened to hear the indistinguishable sound of steel crunching against steel as the frame of the Edsel imploded on itself. Glass windows smashed outwards and the rest of the Edsel twisted, buckled, and was eventually nicely compacted into one flat rectangle resembling a piece of luggage.

"And for next week's event," Bart said to his dwindling, almost non-existent crowd, "we'll be smashing Malto's 1954 elementary school bus. Be sure to come back! You won't want to miss it!"

With tonight's event now apparently over, I helped escort Judge Werner to the awaiting arms of his limousine driver in the parking lot. Then I had the dubious task of rounding up Bully Boy. I hated to admit that was far easier than expected.

But when I opened the old, ill-fitting door to the back storage shed, I stood in shock by the scene playing out in front of me.

A duplicate, perfect mirror-image of Bully Boy stood guard against a big, heavily-built dude plastered flat against the side wall. Lying on the floor I saw a stack of tools protruding from a black canvass bag that it appeared he intended on stealing.

"Ah-ha!" I thought, "Here's Bart's pesky petty thief!

Scared for his life with sweat dripping off the lower edge of his big, flabby double chin, I worried if he didn't stop shaking he might bring down the flimsy metal walls of the shed on top of us, but I didn't blame him for shaking. If a Pitty Bull Pinscher had me cornered, I would have been sweating and shaking like Brenda's overloaded and unbalanced washing machine during the spin cycle.

The duplicate Pitty Bull Pinscher's deep gutter growl gave me pause. We hadn't been formally introduced and if it hadn't been for Brenda coming up behind me, I doubt I would have had the balls to do anything. Instead, I ignored the dog slobbering at my feet and I grabbed a hold of the slob, forcing him to his knees. I tied his hands behind his back with a set of plastic handcuffs and turned to Brenda.

"Brenda, sweetie," I whispered. "Call the police." I would have done it myself, but I wasn't up to trusting my voice yet.

Then Bart finally came rushing up to the shed. He grabbed a hold of both Pitty Bull Pinschers and corralled them inside a doggie holding cell in the corner. He turned to me.

"Justin! I can't believe it! You caught him!"

"Ah, ah," I stammered. I wanted to explain that I hadn't done anything, that the duplicate Pitty Bull Pinscher deserved all the credit. But when Brenda came up and hugged me, worshipping me with her eyes, I did something completely dishonorable—I smiled back at her and I kept the credit for myself.

On my next day on the job at Malto Junk Yard, Bart offered me a reward, the first pick of a robust litter of eight-week-old Pitty Bull Pinscher puppies. And I knew instantly what I would give Brenda for her birthday . . . a puppy who would grow up to protect her whenever I wasn't around.

When Brenda saw what was inside the over-sized crate I struggled to get through the doorway to her apartment, she started making such a big huge fuss; but not over the puppy, over me. From the small oval hallway mirror I saw my face getting red and blotchy, and I must confess the sight of a grown man blushing isn't worth the cost of a Polaroid. Then Brenda handed me the biggest piece of her birthday cake, one topped with pink sugary frosting formed into the shape of rose buds, and I stood in the corner stuffing my face while Brenda cried and ogled over the puppy.

What, I worried, would I do for an encore next year?

A PITY CRYING SHAME

I hate to admit it, but after a long time in coming I was a wreck. I had an ever-expanding bald spot resembling a dry-and-cracked section of the parking lot pavement loosely interspersed with small tufts of wild, dried out weeds, and each year my feet became wider and flatter than an old tire abandoned on the side of the expressway at five o'clock rush hour. And now, after many months of dating Brenda and her doting on me hand and foot with one tasty culinary delicacy after another, like those little apricot-filled Kolacky cookies sprinkled with powdered sugar, I started gaining weight.

The top button of the trousers to my security uniform threatened not to close. After dinner each night, it adamantly refused.

I didn't have the heart, or the stomach, to tell Brenda to stop pampering me. Therefore, the only alternative to regaining my irresistible masculine physique was to exercise like Brenda.

Within the past six months since I met this wonderful new lady in my life, she had redesigned, reshaped, and reinvented herself into a real, honest-to-goodness hottie patatie. I swear now that she wore skinny size-twelve short shorts, I started the practice of scanning newspaper advertisements for a shotgun to keep other guys from stealing her out from underneath me.

But truthfully, as I had a compulsion to remain a sweet, lovable, peace-keeping dude, I knew I had to find some other way to ensure I deserved Brenda's attraction.

I checked out the assortment of exercise equipment Brenda had spread out on her living room floor. She had weights of every size and color, dumbbells, barbells, and weight-lifting bars spread across the top of door jams. She had a treadmill, a teeny-tiny trampoline, and an industrial-sized Master Stair-Stepper to boot. Thank goodness I hadn't been asked to haul that monstrosity up two flights of stairs because I didn't have the back muscles for it.

Stored off to the side, Brenda had a super humungous purple plastic ball that from time to time she would lay on top and slowly swivel around until I got a hard on and was forced to drag her into the bedroom kicking, screaming, and laughing hysterically.

You'll have to take my word for it, but a romp in the sack with me uses up a lot more calories than rolling around on top of a purple ball. And it's a whole lot more fun too.

If you don't believe me, just ask Brenda.

Instead of floor exercises, I decided to be cool like the other guys in the neighborhood who went jogging in the wee hours of the morning wearing fashionable designer sleeveless jerseys and flimsy neopropylene shorts with white strips down the side. Complementing their awesome body-building image, they would sport headphones and plastic squirt bottles. I know because I would stare and wonder about where they got all that energy to prance up and down at stop lights with the agility of a Clydesdale on parade.

But as I don't possess the pizzazz or coolness to compete on their level, I donned an old tee-shirt with the picture of a timber wolf spread across my chest and a pair of cut-off blue jeans with a frayed hem, and I took off running with our puppy, Baby Sweet Cheeks, at my side.

Baby Sweet Cheeks may have looked like a blood-thirsty she-devil, but we loved her intensely. She was the friendliest, sweetest puppy this side of Malto Animal Shelter. She loved giving out big slurpy kisses, but she never got a chance to give more than one. That's because before she could, you were busy looking for a hand towel to dry off the first one.

In other words, I never regretted the day Bart Bartholomew handed her over to me.

I strongly recommend you check into getting a Pitty Bull Pinscher for yourself, but one word of advice. Don't get into the habit of letting them sleep in your bed. They snore worse than I do.

As a part of my exercise plan, Baby Sweet Cheeks and I canvassed the streets of Malto early each morning. We sprinted from Richmond High on the south, twelve blocks to Mannington Avenue on the east, and back again. We clomped on concrete, stumbled on crumbling asphalt, and crunched on loose gravel as we kept an eye out for the sun to come up over the hill and blind us silly.

We couldn't travel too fast because I was a little worried about Baby Sweet Cheeks' bulging puppy belly swaying farther and farther from side to side. Any farther and she'd keel over like a two-ton motorcycle unable to be up-righted by its lanky, underdeveloped owner—the main reason I hadn't ever owned one myself.

I soon discovered that unlike guys who had a tail-wagging black lab puppy, nobody stopped to ask to pet a Pitty Bull Pinscher. In fact, young single women would deliberately cross the street to keep away from us. If they saw us, little kids would start to cry and grab with outstretched arms for their human caretakers.

That really was a pity crying shame because Baby Sweet Cheeks would have loved to clean off their little Kool-Aid kissers. Of course, there was also the risk she'd knock 'em down in the process, so we kept our distance.

The rewarding aspect of our walk was coming back by way of Cell Tower Park and helping ourselves to big gulps of fresh, cold water from the pump. I learned the hard way I had to get my drink first and then stand far away from Baby when she drank from the portable, foldable plastic bowl I kept inside my pocket for occasions like this.

Trust me, you don't want to be anywhere close to a Pitty Bull Pinscher puppy when she starts shaking her head dripping wet with an excess of cold water and doggie slobber.

DUPPED

Sports activists advocate not taking the same jogging route each day in order to protect yourself from your routine pattern being detected by an ill-intentioned bystander. I considered that advice before concluding an overweight security guard traveling with a mutt like Baby Sweet Cheeks generally makes an undesirable target. What would anyone have wanted with us?

Besides, my irregular work hours prohibited me from following any type of normal routine, jogging or any other kind. It was any wonder that the love of my life, Brenda, had been so kind and understanding. One week we'd be sharing dinners promptly at six-thirty in the evening, but as inconsistency was my norm, the next week we'd be grabbing a spontaneous meal together sometime between noon and midnight.

51

What bothered me the most when jogging was not being able to offer a helping hand to women unpacking their most recent haul from garage sales, or to offer a kind word to a little kid who had fallen from his tricycle and scraped his knee. Like it or not, in my role as a jogger I had become the proverbial 'stranger.'

Ah, come on, I wanted to yell. We're talking about me, Justin Maximilian here! Security Guard Extraordinaire!

That's why, when I saw an attractive young woman running towards me in distress, I looked up and took notice.

"Help! Please help!" she screamed. When she got a little closer, I heard her say, "My boyfriend is trapped underneath his car!"

I didn't hesitate. I began running after her like a superhero. I chased her half-way down the hill, about the length of two long city blocks, until she disappeared into the doorway of a rundown warehouse and I did likewise.

Looking back on it, that was a pretty dumb move, even for someone as gullible as me.

I ran straight into the open arms of a group of bandits, otherwise these days known as muggers. Before I had a chance to focus on what was going on, they rushed me. One threw a hood over my head, one grabbed my arms and started wrapping my wrists with duck tape, and yet another poked a gun smack into my solar plexus.

I let go of Baby's leash and was prepared to die on the spot.

A guy's strong, masculine hands roughly rummaged through my pockets, making a straight-laced guy like me feel a bit violated.

I knew from inside my old tattered wallet he'd come across the change left over from my chocolate latte that morning, seven one-dollar bills and twenty-nine cents. Say what! Was I being mugged for a measly seven dollars and twenty-nine cents? What would my muggers think when they found out? Take their revenge out on me?

Oh, darn, I ostracized myself. Why hadn't I thought to carry an extra twenty with me!

Of all the roughing up I was getting, nothing compared to the trauma I was experiencing inside that scratchy burlap sack. I couldn't get enough air to breathe and was rapidly becoming overwhelmed with the gagging smell of a thick, musty mold that, once inhaled, permeated to my lungs and instantly caused a nasty build-up of phlegm. No matter what they had planned beforehand, I knew these guys hadn't intended for me to die of lung congestion. But at that moment I was at a loss to convey what was happening to me.

My next conscious thought was the realization they were taking the bulging key chain out of my side pocket, and a sense of panic overcame me. From my esteemed position as security guard, I had keys to several local businesses, including the master key to the front door of Oxford Shopping Mall. But among all those keys was the most precious of all my belongings—the key to Brenda's apartment. Would these gangbangers have the audacity to go to Brenda's apartment? To hurt her?

"Please God," I prayed, "don't let them hurt Brenda."

That was my last conscious thought because one of the muggers pistol wiped the back of my head and I blacked out as my head fell against the concrete floor.

Coming to was slow going.

Afraid of being hit again, I waited as long as I could before doing anything. Then the exasperating pounding in my head started becoming unbearable. My eyes started watering and I couldn't refrain from coughing up excess phlegm.

That's when I noticed something odd. I opened my eyes and figured out I wasn't wearing that makeshift hood anymore, nor were my hands tied behind my back. As a matter of fact, besides the huge, throbbing goose egg on the back of my head, there wasn't a single piece of hardcore evidence to corroborate the ordeal I had just been through. That's when I realized I had just been duped by some of the nastiest of all hoodlums. The worst kind. Professional thugs.

I was left abandoned in the warehouse, castoff like a lone lost shoe left in the middle of the road. Where do all those shoes come from anyway?

Eventually I brought myself up to a kneeing position and I slowly surveyed the warehouse. Along the side walls, I noticed a few rusting metal tables, an assortment of discarded cardboard boxes, and cartons of empty beer bottles. Nothing else. Then I detected something moving in the far back.

"Baby, come here Baby," I said as sweetly as my scratchy baritone voice would allow. "Come here, Baby."

Cowering in the back of the room, she slowly started making her way to me. When I could reach Baby Sweet Cheeks, I scooped her into my arms in one full swoop and cradled her like a small, hurt child. She was alive. I was alive. More than I expected.

I staggered to get up and fought to clear my head. I had something important I needed to do. Now what was it? Brenda? Oh, yeah, I had to rescue Brenda! As a security guard I may have blundered a few times, but I would never let anything happen to Brenda. Like a track star, I braced and then jet propelled myself off my left foot and tore down the street like a possessed military commando.

Baby Sweet Cheeks did her best to keep up with me, but this time I mercilessly didn't worry about her swaggering belly.

As it turns out Brenda was okay, but I continued to be plagued with ugly flashbacks of my ordeal. From the big stack of Double Dare Detective Magazines on my nightstand, which I read to help counteract my insurgent case of insomnia, I knew all too well how post-traumatic stress disorder can impact people's normal lives. Like any other victim, fear gripped me each time I reached for the doorknob to the front door of the apartment building. Everywhere I looked, I glanced over my shoulder. Every person I saw on the street, I assumed was out to get me.

But then, hey, isn't that normal security guard behavior?

Still, I couldn't let it go. Determined to make a difference, I signed up for lessons at the shooting range. Maybe I would start working out on Brenda's exercise equipment after all.

My days of playing security guard were over.

I could recall every intimate detail of that young woman's small, anemic body. She had long blonde hair brushing past her short, petite shoulders. Her huge blue eyes were wide, round, and held a counterfeit expression of urgency. She wore slicked-up, sparkling pink lip gloss that glistened in the sun, nicely contrasting against her machine-induced suntan. She had grace and agility; tight oblique butt muscles capable of speeding downhill. More specifically, she wore jeans with a sequin design on the backside and size-six black Mary Jane shoes with little leather straps across the top.

I could have easily portrayed her image to a police station sketch artist, but I didn't. I didn't get the police involved at all. I wanted to scope this case by myself, to come up behind her someday and surprise the bejebies out of her like the gangbangers had done to me. I'd twirl her around, slap a pair of handcuffs on her skinny wrists, and drag her down to the local precinct in a retaliatory citizen's arrest. It'd be sweet. Sweet, sweet revenge.

But there was one nagging question that still remained. Could I catch her before this nasty group of gangbangers tried this stunt again on some other innocent, unsuspecting person? Before someone got hurt worse than the throbbing bruise to the back of my head, to say nothing of my aching and bruised ego?

Each morning as Baby Sweet Cheeks and I jogged through the neighborhood, I periodically glanced over my shoulder, studied the intentions of the faces that crossed my path, and made mental note of the types and locations of vehicles on the street. In other words, I assumed the position of a real live detective. How cool was that!

I became the eyes and ears of the neighborhood. I paced back and forth and gave an evil eye to anyone who appeared to be loitering in front of doorways. I made special note of garage doors left open or more than a day's worth of newspapers sitting on the curb. Like homicide detective Lieutenant Columbo, I felt the pulse, the tempo of the city, like it was my own heartbeat, and I was prepared to react if and when the need arose. But I hadn't taken into account how down-and-out obvious I was until the day an official Malto postal carrier came up to ask *me* for directions. Hmmmm. Incognito I wasn't. That needed to change.

I took myself to Joshua Styling Center to reinvent myself.

This was the type of place where they catered and fussed over their customers, offering free drinks of your choice and then doting on you with a wide selection of reading materials including O and GQ.

"O my," I thought. "How much is all this going to cost?"

I met with an official hair design consultant who created various computer-generated graphics with mug shots of me implanted smack in the middle. I got to see myself up close and personal as a gothic rock star like Mick Jagger, a big-bucks millionaire like Bill Gates, and a swav-and-sophisticated business tycoon like Donald Trump. The consultant gave me a sideways question-mark look when I said I wanted to look like a good-for-nothing street punk.

"I've got a job interview as an undercover agent with the CIA," I lied.

"You want a diamond stud in your nose and tats on your upper arms?" he asked.

I was stymied. Would it be necessary to do something that permanent? Before I came up with my decision, the consultant rescued me by offering glued-on imitations. Hmmmm. Maybe that would work! Four and a half hours later, I smiled when I took a look-see in the mirror. My own mother wouldn't recognize me. I couldn't wait to see Brenda's reaction.

But I wasn't done with my new personification re-creation. I took myself on a little clothes shopping spree to Good Will. Oversized jeans, a heavy metal tee-shirt, and a black leather jacket transformed me into a radical street-wise dude with a pair of clunky black leather shoes.

Hey, come on, you can't really expect I'd find a cool pair of extra-wide, size eleven-and-a-half, punk rock boots for next to nothing at Good Will. Can you? My security guard shoes would have to do for now, but I don't think they deterred from my new image.

"Brenda! Ohhhh, Brenda, I'm home!"

SKIDDING AROUND TOWN

Homeland Security may have posted the terrorist attack level on orange, or red, or whatever other color palette they decided that month, but right here, right now, Oxford Shopping Mall's crisis was the shortage of local customers with deep pockets. Or any size pockets at all. In other words, my security guard hours were now cut down to zilch.

Needing to supplement my income in order to maintain the lifestyle in which I had been accustomed, like being able to afford a supersized batch of French fries to go with my Big Mac, I searched the internet for another part-time, flexible job.

"All right!" If I played my cards right, I just might get the position of a taxi driver at Skidd's Taxi Service.

I opened my Microsoft Word file, brushed off the grammatical cob webs from my illustrious resume, and pressed the send button before I had a chance of second-guessing my offer to spending long tedious hours waiting on the happenchance someone had car trouble in Malto, Ohio.

Getting ready for my first job interview in several years took a bit of effort. First, I had to peel off the fake diamond stud stuck to the underside of my nose and I had to apply hot water and soap to the tattoo of an anchor like Popeye's from my left upper forearm. Sadly, I must admit I didn't have the appropriate size of arm muscles to show it off anyway.

I scrounged around the back of my closet until I found the gray tweed suit I had worn to my sister Eloise's wedding four years earlier. There's nothing like a wedding, a funeral, or a job interview to get your wardrobe in order. Having cleverly transformed myself back into a somewhat average-looking, honest-to-goodness trustworthy prospective employee, I hurried to my interview.

"Good defensive drivers like me are hard to come by," Myles Skidd was saying. "For example, take the big snow back in '67. Forty-two inches fell in two days and I was still out there driving the streets like it was a Sunday morning in July. Yes, siree, that's the kind of driver we need here at Skidd's Taxi Service."

"I'm a good driver," I said in defense of myself.

"Yeah, ya know, most people panic at the first sign of inclement weather, but us down here at Skidd's, we're ready and rearing to go whenever the need arises. Now THAT'S a motto worth living up to!"

"Yes, sir, I'm ready and rearing to go," I reiterated.

When all his questions were asked, answered, and accounted for, at least to my satisfaction, Myles opened his office door to send me on my way. Still sitting in the front room and waiting for an interview was an elderly woman most likely needing to supplement her insufficient social security check and a teenage boy who appeared young enough to have just been issued his first driver's license.

I felt pangs of guilt knowing I'd probably have a much better shot at getting the job than they did. That was unfortunate because unlike either one of them, I didn't have a natural gift of gab nor did I have the tenacity to stand up to a client attempting to re-negotiate the fee to the train station.

But when Myles Skidd called to offer me the job, I was in the midst of an intimate moment with Brenda, not affording me the right opportunity to decline his generous job offer. I quickly accepted the job and hung up the phone. Then I re-wrapped my arms around Brenda, stared into her beautiful brown eyes, and said, "Nowww where were we?"

Skidd's Taxi Service had two vehicles in their fleet, a Dodge mini-van and an older Mercedes sedan. For consistency sake, both of them had been painted lime green, Malto's official color.

On my first day on the job, however, one of the taxis was in the shop for engine repairs, so I was assigned an ancient relic of a yellow station wagon decorated with a brown wooden belt circled around its midline. The tires were fairly decent, but the muffler was shot. To my chagrin so was the AM radio.

I drove to the official designated taxi parking spot at the commuter train station and was preparing to close my eyes for a little siesta when I got my first call to duty. It was Brenda. Brenda?

"Oh, Justin," she laughed. "You'll never guess what happened to me!"

Seconds later I was roaring and sputtering my way back to Provincial Garden's parking lot to get a first-hand look at Brenda's flat tire.

"Where's your spare?" I asked after opening the trunk to her car.

"Spare what?"

"Ah," I hesitated. "Hop in. I'll give you a ride to the card shop."

Twenty minutes, one kiss, and fifteen of my dollars later, I was back at the train station when I got a call for yet another fare. Hmmmm. Looks like the taxi cab business was up. I shoved the station wagon into gear and headed to a somewhat shamble of a house located on the outskirts of town—out amongst the big, wide open cornfields of which this part of Ohio is known.

When I arrived, I got out of the taxi and started walking towards the house when a young, heavy-set woman came hobbling and wobbling her way towards me with a suitcase in tow. Was she running away from home? I hoped not. I wouldn't want to be accused of aiding and abetting.

"My water broke!" she said.

I stood there looking dumbfounded until she placed her right hand flat on her protruding stomach and said, "I'm having a baby! Let's get to the hospital!"

"Yes, of course!" I responded in shock.

No sooner did she get inside the backseat of my taxi substitute when she started moaning and wailing something awful. Terrified, I turned the key in the ignition and was prepared to break the sound barrier all the way to the hospital, but my ears became overwhelmed with the reverberating sound of my foot pumping the gas pedal without a response from the engine.

Then the woman read my mind because she started yelling "help!"

"Yes!" I thought. "I'm going to have to call for help!"

Then I must admit I had thoughts of running across open cornfields to the nearest farmhouse when a very loud voice demanded that I get into the backseat with her. Oh, no. Did I hear that right?

Hey. What do you take me for? I'm Justin Maximilian here. Security Guard Extraordinaire. I'm not a fireman! Not a paramedic!

"Hurry! It's coming!"

I gingerly opened the back door, squinted my eyes in a gesture of privacy, and held out my arms. Seconds later a very wet and slippery little guy slid into my arms and I was completely awestruck. He was the most beautiful, most adorable, sweetest little person ever to be born and right then and there I lost my heart and soul. My head was spinning and it took a moment for me to comprehend someone was speaking to me.

"What is it? A boy or a girl?"

"A boy!" I exclaimed in pride. "A perfectly wonderful little boy!"

A short time later an ambulance came whizzing into the driveway and ushered my instant new family away from me. I stood on the driveway watching them pull away, getting farther and farther away by the minute. I felt wounded, empty and abandoned.

"Justin!" Brenda said in her attempt to console me later that night, "You're a hero!"

"No, no. I'm not."

"Oh, yes, you are! And get ready because we're going to the hospital to go see the baby!"

"We are?"

Leading me through the corridors with a series of lefts and rights and an elevator ride or two, Brenda pushed me into a pane of glass to see a row of newborn babies all wrapped up like tiny sleeping mummies that, unlike the Egyptians, were placed in clear plastic storage bins from Wal-Mart.

"Look!" Brenda said, "There's the little boy who was born earlier today!"

And there he was. I would recognize those tiny squinty eyebrows and upturned nose anywhere. I stood staring and smiling at him when Brenda announced, "Justin look. He's named after you!"

"Maximilian Timothy Granger" read the label on the front of his plastic bin.

Love struck as much as I was with little baby Maximilian, Brenda got it in her mind for us to hunt down and speak with his mother. Be it not in my nature to argue, we did.

And then I found myself face to face with the young blond woman who had tricked me into getting mugged.

Feeling fairly confident she hadn't recognized me yet, I feigned a happy social demeanor until we left and headed back home.

But I knew I would be awake all night long pondering what to do next. Could I call the police and get her arrested? And leave little Max without a mother?

No way.

CONSPIRING WITH THE ENEMY

Like a powerful magnetic force from the dark side pulling me forward, I felt powerless to keep from driving back to the hospital the next afternoon. I can't explain the bond I felt for my little namesake, but it was irresistible. Relentlessly I canvassed the hospital hallways until eventually was I was standing at Lisa Granger's bedside as she cradled Maximilian in her arms.

"Hi," she said. "He's beautiful, isn't he?"

"Yes," I agreed.

"He's like a breath of fresh air."

"Yes, he is."

"A brand-new person and he's all mine, a chance for me to start over to set things right."

"And his father?" I asked.

"He's not in the picture," she explained. "That didn't work out too well."

"You don't recognize me, do you?" I blurted.

I watched Lisa's face making the transition from peace and tranquility of a new mother into someone traumatized with fear and anxiety. Her arms hugged baby Max a little tighter.

"Oh! You're, you're . . ."

"Yes. I am. I thought maybe we could talk?"

She looked at me with large round eyes threatening to spill over with tears and I was able to detect a spark of sincerity and remorse that I hadn't seen last summer when she lured me into that garage. Maybe, just maybe, I thought, in all good consciousness I might be able forgive her and not have her hauled off to jail like I originally intended.

"But the others," I began, "have they seen the error of their ways? Are they still a threat to the community?"

Lisa pressed her lips into a hard, firm line and shook her head sideways.

"I don't know. I haven't seen any of them since last summer, but I suspect unless they've been caught they're still out there someplace. But I need to tell you, Mr. Maximilian, I was, and I still am, so sorry for what happened to you. I know it doesn't help, but I really didn't know they were planning to hurt you."

"So would you be willing to turn their names into the police? To stop them before they really do hurt someone?"

"No! I can't do that! They'd come after me . . . and Max. I can't let that happen!"

Both of us switched our gaze to see baby Maximilian, content and sweetly sleeping, unaware of an outside world plagued with chaos. He pursed his lips together and ever so slightly flexed them in a dream of suckling his mother's breast.

"Hmmm, but Lisa," I hemmed. "We can't let those guys stay out there. We can't risk them hurting someone. We have to do something."

"What if you were to come across them in the act? Then they'd be arrested without me being involved at all. Don't you think? Wouldn't that work?"

"Ah, I thought you didn't know where they were?"

"I don't, but I could help you try to find them. If you wanted me to, that is."

Enter into a conspiracy with Lisa Granger? Start our own secret covert operation? Run around like some kind of adrenaline-crazed undercover cop? Could this be legal? Could this be safe?

"Sure. Why not."

SHOW ME THE MONEY

Fickle Malto residents now ignored the newly-released gloomy consumer confidence index by spending more of their dwindling hard-earned money at Oxford Shopping Mall, bolstering my work hours as a security guard. That was good for me because the sporting season for Bart's Car Crushing Show was now over. However, I still continued to maintain my position as a part-time substitute taxi car driver.

Having another mouth to feed was putting a damper on our monthly food budget.

Each week I had to drag another twenty-pound bag of Crunchy Puppy Chow home to Baby Sweet Cheeks who already had outgrown her padded doggie bed and had to lay with her head and tail draped over each of the sides. It made my back ache just to look at her.

"So, Justin," Brenda said to me, "I have to work at the card shop tonight so it's your turn to take Baby to her puppy classes."

"Puppy classes?"

There were a lot of small dogs, like a Poodle, a Snicker-doodle, and a Shih Tzu. Big dogs included a massive black Newfoundland and a sleek-and-shiny Golden Retriever. While the American Kennel Club didn't recognize a breed like Pitty Bull Pinschers, neither did the puppy owners sitting on the folding chairs placed neatly in a semi-circle. Baby Sweet Cheeks and I kept to ourselves at the far end of the classroom and had to endure occasional sideways glances from the others. Really, I thought, is she really that unusual looking?

I half wished Baby would raise her upper lip to expose her lethal-looking incisors at them, but instead she did something far better. She closely watched my every move and quickly responded to everything asked of her. My hairless chest swelled up with pride and happiness, and I wanted to sneer at the other class attendees even though Baby Sweet Cheeks refused to lower her standards to that extent.

"Good girl!" I said when she laid at my feet in response to my flattened palm. "Good girl!"

After class, Baby smiled sweetly at the portly puppy class teacher as he handed her a well-earned doggie treat. I also decided to treat her so we headed hand-and-leash past the first doggy accessory isle. No sooner had we rounded the corner when Baby started growling and lunging forward, almost jerking her leash out of my hand.

"No! Baby no!" I yelled, not quite sure if she'd heed my command.

Surrounded by a shipment of an odd assortment of dog toys was a twenty-something punk sitting on the floor on his hands and knees. He had a purple-and-orange striated mohawk, the likes of which Native Americans wouldn't have ever imagined years before Columbus started our invasion of their country. How this guy got hired here at Doggy Heaven was anyone's guess.

When Mr. Striated Mohawk heard Baby lunging for his throat, he put up his plastic price label maker in an attempt to protect his pimple-covered face. Then he scrambled to get to his feet and took off running like Roadrunner being chased by Coyote. I could hardly blame him. But before he had turned away from me, I had been able to read his name tag: Marcel.

Marcel? Could this be one and the same Marcel that Lisa Granger had included in the list of muggers from last summer? No wonder, I thought. This is why Baby Sweet Cheeks was so unusually aggressive. She remembered him!

We left Doggy Heaven and I allowed Baby the luxury to sniff and circle the postage-stamp size of artificial green grass in front of the store, but as soon as she was done squatting to pee, I ushered her into the backseat of my car. And, in my attempt to remain hidden from view, I joined her as I kept my eyes focused on the front door of the store. Whenever Marcel got off work, I would be hot on his trail to record the type of car he drove, his license plates, and hopefully his home address. And to think I owed it all to Baby Sweet Cheeks.

"Good girl," I said. "Good girl!"

Next week after puppy classes, I would definitely have to get her a special treat.

The windows to my Volkswagen started getting fogged up and I began to worry that passers-by might become suspicious of a little hanky-panky going on in my backseat, a situation that could completely obliterate my attempt to remain concealed from view. I swiped the coat sleeve of my lower arm across the small side window and that's when I saw him—a red-haired, be-speckled ten-year-old boy standing with his nose pressed against my window.

"Woof! Woof!"

"Baby, down!" I scolded, in my attempt to maintain a semblance of control over the situation.

One look at Baby Sweet Cheeks with her eyes gone wild-mad and a yard of drool hanging down her mouth and the boy took off screaming for his mom. My heart raced as I worried more people would come to accuse me of something sinister like animal cruelty, but after a few minutes of no one materializing before me, I gave up those fears. Then, I almost missed Marcel as he shut the door to an older Mazda and recklessly left via the 'in' entrance.

I hustled to scale over the back of the front seat, a stunt I don't recommend anyone, especially someone six feet tall, try to do from inside a Volkswagen Beatle.

As soon as I shook out the kinks from my lower back, I grabbed the steering wheel and peeled out of the parking lot at a safe distance away. And wouldn't you know it, I followed him to an older high-rise apartment building less than a block away from mine. All this time and I just now found out that we were neighbors! Hmmmm, I thought, maybe I should get the ladies over at Welcome Wagon to pay him a little friendly visit?

Then by coincidence, the next week I came across another one of the guys on Lisa's list.

My spot from inside the taxi afforded me the best opportunity to become the eyes and ears of the city and, unlike jogging my buns off, I was now in a temperature-controlled environment not requiring any physical exertion. Not only was I was getting paid for time off my professional position as a security guard, but I was benefiting from on-the-job training in the fine art of delivering a smooth-and-polished line of customer service lingo to taxi patrons. The tape measurement I used to plot my progress was from the size of my tips which I protectively horded for a future rainy day.

They say you get what you ask for. It seems today I did. Thunder storms tormented me all day as I sloshed from one fare to another. The weather put everyone in a foul mood. I only had $4.65 to show for my efforts; the sixty-five cents coming from underneath the back seat. But still, it was a good day because I got my first good lead about the whereabouts of Terrence Rudesby, one of the alleged muggers.

"Drop me off at Egads," the young man directed me.

"Really?" I said. "That's only four blocks away."

"Hey, man! It's pouring out there."

"True enough."

I peered at him through my slightly-slanted rearview mirror. He was wearing dreadlocks past his shoulders and chomping on a wad of bubble gum. His swaying and gyrating to the beat of the music from his earphones made me suspect he might be a fare runner. Go ahead and try it, I thought to myself. If he did, I'd jump out of the car, pin him to the ground, and press his face in a mud puddle. Humph. It seems I was in a foul mood today like everybody else.

"You related to those Rudesby boys?" I asked.

"What you saying? I *am* one of the Rudesby boys," he responded with a splash of righteousness.

"How about Terrence? Is he still working at Subway?"

"Naw," he said. Then he starred back at me through the rearview mirror, judging me. "You know Terrence?

"We used to shoot pool back in the day," I lied.

The guy nodded his head. Whether to acknowledge me or in response to his music I wasn't sure.

"He's in Shipping and Receiving at Montgomery Ward. It's a sweet gig if you're looking to change jobs."

"Yo!" I said, "Look at me. I'm sitting here in the lap of luxury."

"Yeah, whatever. Here, keep the change."

He got out of the car and found myself looking at President Lincoln. I guess I should have been grateful to receive a full twenty-five cent tip. After all, as rumor has it, Lincoln walked two miles to return some guy's two cents change. Factoring inflation, it was the same difference. But the satisfaction I felt knowing how to locate Terrence Rudesby was tip enough.

The problem with getting away with a crime, as I see it from personal observation, is that you get this over-inflated impression you can't get caught. Then things continue escalating to bigger and better things. If only a guy would sit down and have a little talk with himself and say, "Hey, I've been pressing my luck so it's high time I quit."

Time was of the essence. I had to catch this mugging trio before they took to the streets again; before they had a chance to hurt someone else.

PARTY HEARTY

We got the bad news by way of invitation.

Bill Taylor's divorce from Sue was final.
But according to the glossy card we just received
in the mail, Bill wasn't too broken up about it. He
was planning a special event to celebrate, a
divorce party.

I couldn't wait. Not because of
anticipation of the party, but because Brenda had
made her revolving relish tray that she called her
'Lazy Susan.'

Call me lazy or call me hungry, but it was
hard for me to keep from extending my
oversized, calloused knuckles to gobble up those
tempting hors d'oeuvres in one sitting. Cocktail
wieners, cold-boiled shrimps, salami slices, and
cubes of sharp cheddar competed for available
dish space and my salivary glands started working
overtime like one of Pavlov's hound dogs. The
poor mutts. Did Pavlov share his Nobel peace

prize with any of them? Offer them a steak dinner? Provide them with a doggie bed by the open fire? Nope, I doubt it.

But Chef Boyardee, Bill wasn't. Knowing his handiwork of grilling chicken within a fraction of the bone marrow didn't get me any too hopeful anything besides Brenda's relish tray would be worth drooling over at the party. Now if Sue had been invited, it would have been entirely different.

But Sue was at the party.

She was all over the place, from the little framed picture of herself on the half-round table in the front vestibule, to the life-sized oil positioned over the fireplace mantle. Frilly floral pillows were piled high on the couch and lacey drawback sheers outlined the living room windows. And the bathroom countertop had an assortment of little colored bottles of who-knows-what and a formally-dressed porcelain cat standing guard over the toilet bowl scrubber.

Either Sue left in a big hurry or was planning to come back later to get her stuff.

After awhile, Bill's place started getting too crowded with divorce-well-wishers and I was thinking of escaping to the basement or the garage when I unexpectedly bumped into Louie, my apartment manager.

"Louie? I didn't expect to see you here. How do you know Bill?"

"Oh, hello, Justin. I've known Bill ever since that mishap over at the car crushing show. We got better acquainted spending time together inside one of the port-a-potties."

"Inside the port-a-potty?"

"Oh, yes sir. Weren't many other places available to get away from that rabid dog, you know?"

"Ug, yeah, I guess," I replied.

"And Justin, it's such good timing to see you. I need you to meet Serena, my intended bride."

Louie ushered me through the mingling crowd which was busy munching on helpings from Brenda's relish tray. We stopped in front of a short, thin woman who, like a character in foreign film, had a dot glued to the center of her forehead and was encased in a bolt of shimmering bejeweled fabric with a remnant encircling the top of her head.

"Serena traveled all the way from India to meet me," Louie said proudly. "An arranged marriage set up by my father."

"Arranged marriage?" I repeated incredulously. Did they arrange weddings for forty-year-old bachelors like Louie? Apparently so. Then I looked up to see another older Indian woman standing close by.

"And this is Mrs. Gupta," Louie said. "She's here as Serena's escort to make sure I don't prematurely take advantage of my bride-to-be."

Louie laughed, but I refrained from chuckling or otherwise making a fool of myself, which I wasn't sure I pulled off. But I did have the presence of mind to ask, "When's the wedding?"

"Oh, there's much planning still needs to be done," Louie said. "Maybe in a year or two if we're lucky."

"Lucky? That's lucky?" I questioned myself.

My stomach gurgled while out from the corner of my eye, I watched Mrs. Gupta reaching for the last of Brenda's hors d'oeuvres. Then, headed on his way outside the back door, Bill waltzed past me with a large platter of raw chicken in his left hand and a voluptuous blonde clinging to the other.

I shook my head in disbelief. Didn't Bill know that women like Brenda were the real deal?

FAMILY TIES

From the moment I first saw him, I was enraptured with little baby Maximilian. He was the perfect spitting image of a newborn, the reason I always wear a diaper draped across my shoulder each time I pick him up. And I forsake any and all pretense of showing the rough-and-tough side of me, or what little of it I still possess, by being reduced to unexpectedly saying things like, "cutchie coo." Cutchie coo? Where did that come from?

My only problem was being able to get my fair share of free time with Max. Once she heard of the struggles Lisa Granger had been through, Brenda took over. She started cooking meals for Lisa, babysat for Lisa, and began designing a series of computer literacy classes for Lisa. In between times, Brenda expertly fed and diapered Max, gathered more and more garage-sale toys and baby equipment for him, and never let a minute go by without telling him a long and steady line of how much she loved him.

Hey! Hey! What about me? Don't I count anymore?

Instead of being accosted with hugs and kisses when I arrived at Brenda's apartment each night or being served hand-and-foot with my favorite appetizers or smells of roasted beef stew slowly simmering in the crock pot, I had to take a number, get at the end of the line, and wait my turn.

But did I get my head out of joint or go running to spend more time down at the pool hall? Become a television football fanatic? Seek the love and attention of another woman? No, of course not! I knew that eighteen or twenty years from now, once Brenda's young new boyfriend grew up and started dating other women, I'd get her back again. Until then, I'd be patiently waiting. So I focused on my new pastime—

investigating and ultimately catching my newly-found muggers engaged in a criminal act.

But I knew Marcel and Terrance were nothing short of small-town, petty criminals. The third one, Braxton, had to be the instigator of this group and I wouldn't be able to finalize my mission until I was able to get him identified. To do so, I did exactly what both criminals and criminal investigators do alike: I went back to the scene of the crime.

The rundown warehouse where I had been mugged last summer was right where I had left it, sitting in the middle of the block on Harrison Avenue. Except this time the center garage door, as well as the small service door, were locked and bolted shut without any clue as to whom, if anyone, would be back. Nor did I see any other neighboring business owners loitering in the vicinity. I decided to conduct a title search down at the courthouse. When the county clerk accessed the owner on record and wrote it down for me, my heart did a back flip when I saw it. The owner was none other than the owner of Malto Junk Yard, the originator of the Car Crushing Show, the infamous Bart Bartholomew. Bart couldn't be involved in anything as sinister as local muggings, but thinking again, could there possibly be a connection to him?

"Justin! How are you Justin!"

"Fine. Fine. I'm good."

"And how's Baby Sweet Cheeks? She's a real sweetie pie of a lap dog just like Bully Boy, isn't she?"

I smiled. Bart had me there.

"Hey, Bart. What can you tell me about that old warehouse on Harrison? Do you own that? What's it used for?

Bart took a minute to respond to my question and then, probably because of my sophisticated interrogation style, he bellied up and said, "Oh, I've leased that to my nephew, Braxton Bartholomew."

Braxton? I gulped. "When did you do that?"

"Been going on for three, four years. Why? What's up?

"I've been helping my friend find some storage space," I guiltily lied. "Do you know what Braxton's doing with the space? How long he's thinking of keeping it?"

"Not sure. Come to think of it, it's been a long while since I've seen him. I'll have to get in touch with him."

"Can you give me his number?"

I followed Bart into his ratty-tatty office and watched him scrowl through a Rolodex. The cards had bent corners and were covered with dirty smudges of black fingerprints. Then with thick, calloused fingers with creases permanently smudged with grease and grime, Bart wrote down a number on the back of a sales flyer and handed it to me.

"Can't say for sure that's still his number."

"I'll try it out. Thanks."

Comforted that Bart wasn't a part of Braxton's shenanigans, I headed back home to see if I could dig up any more dirt about Braxton on-line, a ready source of information these days.

And, as my stomach was reminding me, it was dinnertime. Maybe Brenda was back to her old ways, cooking up a storm in the kitchen? And ready for a little lovin' later tonight? I sure hoped so because just like her sweet-and-spicy barbeque chicken, Brenda was oh-so finger-licking good.

SINCERELY YOURS

Winter that year started early like a hungry lion roaring his head off, and he didn't appear ready to leave anytime soon. Even Grumpy, our local infamous groundhog, didn't poke his head out of his den on Ground Hog Day, making front-page headline news in Malto for three days in a row.

Cold snowy weather and groundhogs notwithstanding, Brenda was oblivious to anything and everything around her while she was up to her elbows in sorting and stacking Valentine's Day cards down at Sincerely Yours Card Shop. She would leave the apartment at sunup and not get back home until well past sundown, leaving me the daunting responsibility of preparing dinner. Not wanting to risk Brenda losing her identity as our culinary expert, I stuck to simple meals like frozen fish sticks and canned peas. Oh yum.

Brenda hinted that perhaps on Saturday morning I should come to the card shop to give her a helping hand. Of course, as Security Guard Extraordinaire I picked up on her subtle comment and thought about immediately volunteering to come to her rescue, but I was scared all the way down to my in-grown toenails. Back in my bachelor days I had tried my hand at playing poker and had routinely embarrassed myself by not being able to master the art of shuffling cards. So I preferred, thank you very much, to stand five feet away from cards whether they be in the form of Old Maid, Black Jack, or Happy Birthday cards.

Every once in a while, though sometimes a little too frequently for my comfort, Brenda intercedes on behalf of my phobias to set me straight.

"Hey, Justin! You have to say 'yes.' I really need your help!"

But since sitting inside a taxi cab and freezing my thumbs off sounded more appealing than sorting red heart-shaped greeting cards, I gave my most sincere apologies to my darling Brenda, along with a big kiss and a hug, and I hurried to scrape off a two-inch layer of ice adhered to the top my windshield. Then, as I worked to help my ailing defroster by repeatedly swiping my glove across the windshield, I listened to a weather report of a deluge of five more inches of skier's delight, bless their little frost-covered eyelashes.

My Volkswagen Beatle predictably fishtailed itself across town and slid into a parking spot at Skidd's Taxi Service, where it patiently waited for two hours until Myles Skidd admitted the citizens of Malto had wised up and elected not to brave the elements. So after employing the aid of a pair of jumper cables attached to the Volkswagen battery, I was juiced up and well on my way to the card shop after all.

A little tinkle bell above the door announced my arrival.

Looking perplexed, Brenda was standing behind the counter while a lethal-looking, four-foot-tall senior citizen wearing an odd assortment of clothes from the 50's and 60's spouted about having bought one of those music-enhanced cards which crashed and burned just before the time of giving. And upon hearing Brenda's offer to give her another one free of charge, this gray-haired fashion disaster continued with her rampage.

"Well, I've never before needed a 'Congratulations on Your New Home' card, and it's highly doubtful I'll ever need one of those again, so that's not going to help me! Do you THINK?"

I quickly sized up the situation because I, too, was mesmerized with those music-type cards and couldn't resist opening and re-opening them if and when I were to ever walk past one. It was a wonder that card shop owners like Brenda didn't charge by the hour for people to play with them. So, of course it's understandable why the card this woman bought wasn't operational by the time of gift-giving.

Against my better judgment, I was about to recommend the obvious, that she agree to accept a different type of card, when she started up again.

"The moment has come and gone," the woman continued. "So what can you do about that!"

"Well, Valentine's Day is coming up soon," Brenda offered. "Or what if I were to let you pick out two Easter cards instead?"

"Easter? My son is too old to appreciate getting an Easter card unless you were throw in a package of those little candy Easter eggs too?"

Perhaps an even-tempered, rational person would have decided to cut their losses and give this irate woman a bag of candy free of charge, but as Brenda had confided in me, the card business was struggling to avoid having to use red pens on the bottom of their monthly balance sheet. Brenda shook her head 'no' which brought our negotiations to a screeching halt. And then Miss Mix & Match did the unthinkable. She reached inside her purse and brought out a small black pistol that she pointed straight at me.

Brenda screamed and I extended both of my arms straight in the air. Thankfully I was still wearing a Kevlar vest underneath my lime green Skidd's Taxi Service uniform shirt, but I wasn't about offer myself as a test case as to its dependability. Not that I wasn't willing to make the ultimate sacrifice to save the love of my life who was now standing exposed and vulnerable.

Staring at the handgun must have caused me to become a bit cross-eyed because I could have sworn the gun was missing its bullet cartridge. No bullets? But looking at the intensity of the woman's expression was enough to give me pause until I heard a God-awful siren blaring and I realized Brenda had the presence of mind to pull the burglar alarm.

Becoming scared, the woman shifted her focus from side to side whereupon I took it upon myself to fling myself in her direction. The two of us ended sprawled in a heap of flaying arms and legs on the tile floor until I was able to wrestle the gun out of her hand. Now feeling defeated, the woman cowered on the floor and began sobbing as though the top of the cake in her oven had caved in.

"Don't shoot!" she screamed. "Don't shoot!"

I stood up and spun around at the sound of two armed policemen pounding on the door and once again I had my arms extended in the air.

"No!" I heard Brenda screaming. "It's Justin! He's a good guy!"

I felt little bursts of pride swelling up inside of me, and I knew it had all been worth it—until I learned the gun really had been loaded and realized I could have been killed during my little bout of heroics. Feeling faint and weak-kneed, I sunk back to the floor again.

DOG EAT DOG

Sure as hootin' I could tell something was wrong. My security guard instinct was on high alert. Unlike usual, Louie didn't bring the bill for our monthly assessment straight to our door. In return, Brenda didn't have an opportunity to invite him to sit with us at the kitchen table for some crumb cake and hot tea where we'd kill time and talk about nothing. That was unsettling because I was particularly good at doing both: killing time and talking about nothing.

"Hey, Louie," I said the next time I saw him, "What's going on?"

When Louie responded by staring at the floor, shrugging his shoulders, and saying, "nothing," I knew that meant "something." Security guards are pretty perspicacious that way.

So as soon as our next monthly assessment came in the mail, I promptly delivered our check to Louie up front and personal. It was high time we dueled it out together, man to man. However, once I knew what was bothering him, I wished I had let enough alone. I wasn't man enough to face what he had to tell me.

"There have been some complaints," he started, "that you shouldn't be allowed to have such a big dog at the apartment complex."

"Baby Sweet Cheeks? Somebody complained about Baby Sweet Cheeks?"

"Yep, they did."

Walls of gold stripped wallpaper began swirling around me as I had an image of Baby looking up at me with her large, dreamy eyeballs while pounding the tip of her strong, thick tail in a steady drum-beat tempo on the floor. I thought how beautifully she pranced along my side as we jogged through the neighborhood and how delicately gentle she accepted treats from my outstretched hand. Were we talking about the same sweet puppy?

Then Louie's next comment hit me where it hurt the most; squarely in my heart.

"The problem is she's so big and so ugly. People are scared of her."

"Scared of her?"

"Yep, they are."

My image as a tough-guy security guard notwithstanding, I became dizzy and I had to grab onto the edge of Louie's old wooden desk for support. The crux of my world was crumbling at my feet and I was unprepared to save Baby or myself. But from the farthest regions of my brain, I wrestled to come to grips with the first impression I had of Bully Boy and I was now forced to admit Pitty Bull Pinschers are not now, nor will they ever be, a symbol of the family pet. Hands down, Lassies and Benjis they aren't.

"Give me some time to think about that, okay Louie?"

I could now see the error of my ways. Back when Baby Sweet Cheeks was still just a little puppy I should have been busy socializing her with the other tenants of the building; gradually acclimating them to her. I felt that I could still get that done—even if I had to go as far as to hire the dog whisperer who routinely advertised on page three of the Malto Daily Times.

There was no way I would ever part with Baby Sweet Cheeks.

Nor could I envision the time and trouble it would take for Brenda and I to relinquish both of our apartments to move somewhere else. If necessary, I was prepared to square off for an honest-to-goodness, old-fashioned standoff with the other Provincial Garden residents.

Wasn't it still a free world? Let them move out!

UNTIL WE MEET AGAIN

With Baby's strong sense of smell and her long-term memory being so much sharper than mine, I periodically took her for a stroll past Marcel, Terrance, and Braxton's. To outsiders, we appeared to look like any other dog-and-master walk takers, but I knew if Baby ever got an opportunity to come within a sniff or two of our past muggers, she'd start growling and lunging for them something awful. Then I'd know for sure they were our mugging culprits—and the look on their faces would tell it all.

But Brenda didn't see it that way and pleaded for me to give up what she called my 'vendetta.' And no matter how hard I tried, there was no appeasing her.

"But what if they do it again? What if they hurt someone next time?" I said in my defense.

117

"So what if they do?" she would say. "Does that justify stalking them? Putting yourself at risk? What does that prove?"

I was tempted to concede with Brenda's reasoning except for the part about putting myself at risk. What did she think I did every day at work?

When I put on my uniform, I was willingly putting my life on the line to an untold number of unknown circumstances. Marcel, Terrance, and Braxton didn't pose the same level of risk. I knew who they were and what they were likely to do next. And they had no clue as to who I was, especially when I put on my fake handlebar mustache and the big brown mole on my lower chin. Security guards like me are clever that way.

But I must admit that over time I grew tired of my unofficial surveillance. Either I was never at the right time or the right place to catch them in the act or they had now redeemed themselves to be on the up and up.

118

So I gradually adopted Brenda's position after all, which was just fine with Baby Sweet Cheeks as she now had my full and undivided attention each time I took her to Cell Tower Park where I could get in a little ball arm-throwing practice.

Too bad Baby didn't help me out by retrieving my ball. She would just run to it, sniff it, and then sit there waiting for me to run up and fetch it myself. But I didn't complain. Considering the size of her front incisors I figured she'd pretty much tear up my nerf ball before dropping it at my feet.

So life became routine and mundane.

On Wednesday, which apparently was the day of least threat to life and limb at Oxford Shopping Mall, I was looking forward to a day off when I came face to face with Brenda's official To-Do list of errands. After spending a few minutes on Map-Quest-dot-com determining the most efficient route from place to place, I grabbed my coat and headed to the front door only to be stopped by eighty-five pounds of dog flesh. And no matter what I said or tried to do, Sweet Baby Cheeks wouldn't budge from the front door until I smiled and invited her to come along with me.

Hmmm, had she been taking notes from Brenda?

We happily buzzed from place to place, dropping off dry cleaning, picking up six month's worth of flea-and-tick ointment from the vet, and standing in line at Udder Delicious for a tub of Black Licorice Ice Cream which was quickly scaling the top of Baby Sweet Cheek's list of favorites.

All that was left to do was a quick twirl through the drive-up window at the bank to make Brenda's monthly twenty-dollar deposit in her Christmas savings account. Given she was saving for a gift for me, I now had a clear idea as to how much I was expected to spend on her.

Whew! I was mightily relieved of having resolved that dilemma when I realized I had no clue what to get her regardless of the cost. Oh, well, I wouldn't dwell on that. I had until Christmas Eve to make that decision.

After finger tapping the entire Brahms lullaby on my steering wheel, I became a little concerned as to what happened to the drive-up bank teller. Then, according to good old Murphy's Law, the bank attendant came back and was either having the worst day ever or a bad case of Poison Ivy because she started nervously twitching her eyebrows, winking with her right eye, followed by gesturing and jerking of her neck muscles. On the chance whatever condition she had was contagious through the automatic cash drawer, I took a hold of Brenda's deposit slip, gingerly gripped it between my front teeth, and shoved my car into gear and out of the drive-up lane in no time.

I circled around the block but was unable to find a parking spot in front of Cell Tower Park so I settled on a spot across the street—at the bank again—but this time I was lucky enough to grab a parking spot right in front. I'm not generally the lucky type so I must confess I was a little suspicious. But since I didn't want to put a hex on anything bad happening, I chose not to dwell on it.

"Come on, Baby," I said, "I'll give you five minutes to sniff around."

But by the time I locked the car door and turned around, Baby was nowhere to be seen. She wasn't underneath the car or loitering anywhere on the sidewalk. Where could she have gone off?

"Baby! Babbyyyy!" I yelled to no avail.

Perspiration accumulated across my forehead and the underarms of my shirt became soggy as I began pacing back and forth along the sidewalk. Gosh almighty, had somebody dog napped her? Not knowing which direction she might have taken off, I was unable to try to head her off. Instead I stood there worrying with my back braced up against the car door until I heard a bunch of police car sirens screeching and screaming in my direction. They landed right behind me.

"Stick 'em up," yelled one of the officers while pointing his .38 caliber handgun at the center of my chest. Still not accustomed to being on this side of a gun, I froze in place.

"What?" I said.

"Put your hands up and step away from the car," said another policeman.

Thinking that some way, somehow, I could find someone to help me figure all of this out, I turned my head left and then right. But I wasn't fast enough. A young rookie policeman charged head-on, knocking me to the ground. Lucky for both of us, I didn't scuff up a hole in my expensive uniform pants.

"Alright, tell us what's going on around here!"

"Ah, I've lost my dog," I said.

"So you're a smart aleck, huh?" he said as he twirled me around to slap a pair of official stainless-steel handcuffs on me like I was some kind of low-down, common criminal.

"Hey, guys! You can't do that," I yelled. "I'm Justin Maximilian, Security Guard Extraordinaire!"

"And you're not the bank robbers' getaway driver?"

"The WHAT? A getaway driver with an orange Volkswagen Beatle?"

Ha! I laughed to myself. These policemen probably didn't know that my beater Volkswagen could get far better gas mileage than their souped-up glossy white cars with swirly lime-green stripes along the sides. Nonetheless, I intuitively knew it wouldn't be in my best interest to attempt a getaway, planned or not.

But as we worked in the same industry, what I did expect was to be extended a little bit of professional courtesy. While not generally prone to impatient outbursts, I felt a surge of irritability swelling deep inside of me. When I couldn't take it anymore, I surprised the hell out of me and both policemen by hauling off and kicking my foot at the lower side of my car.

Then that stunt of mine backfired when my foot smashed straight through-and-through the rusted side panel. And try as I might, my foot became embedded and I was unable to retract it. Now having embarrassed myself enough for a lifetime, I was forced to endure even further humiliation because in order to prevent myself from keeling over to the ground, I had to repeatedly hop on my other foot like the time my sister insisted I participate in a three-legged race with her. That didn't turn out much better than the predicament I was in now; it took both of the officers to rescue me by helping me to pull my foot out.

Just then the front door to the bank bust open and the first person I noticed was Henry Stetson, the bank president. He stuck his head outside the door and yelled.

"Hey, guys! Come on in! We got 'em!"

I was quickly thrown into the back of a patrol car without any further hoopla and had to tough it out alone until some of the officers started filing back out of the bank with big grins on their faces. The first one who I had spoken before came to the car, opened the door, and asked me if I was the owner of the world's most ugly dog.

"Hey, come on!" I said defensively, "you can't call Baby Sweet Cheeks that!"

"Hold on there buddy," he responded as he began relieving me of those God-awful handcuffs. "Your 'baby' just foiled a bank robbery in progress. Just might get herself a reward or her picture in the paper."

"Baby Sweet Cheeks did that?"

"Yeah. Here they come now."

I began watching a procession of police officers filing out the bank with the alleged bank robbers in tow. Wouldn't you know, it was none other than Marcel, Terrence, and Braxton.

And bringing up the end of the line with her head held high and her tail wagging like a flag on the fourth of July was my Baby Sweet Cheeks, Attack Doggie Extraordinaire.

In the split second I had looked the other way, Baby had spotted our muggers, followed them inside the bank, and held them at bay until the police got there.

What a doggie!

"Hey, sorry about that," the young officer apologized for mistakenly identifying me as one of the bad guys.

"It could happen to anyone," I said, even though that was one mistake I hadn't yet made myself.

REWARD ENOUGH

Last winter a red Christmas candle sitting on the windowsill of the Marvin Tatterson home on Skylark Avenue lit the curtains on fire. The whole house was engulfed in flames before the Malto Fire Department could get there. By then Marvin, his wife, and two of their kids were standing in their pre-arranged meeting place by the antique-looking street lamp awaiting rescue.

Like so many other enfolding crises of today, a passerby captured the scene on his cell phone video recorder just when Peggy Tatterson began screaming, "Where's Trevor!"

Immediately the video became a blur as the amateur cameraman shifted his focus to the front doorway where a heroic fireman appeared with two-year-old Trevor's arms wrapped tight around the firefighter's neck. A cheer from neighbors erupted as Trevor was passed safe and sound into his mother's arms.

Mesmerized from repeatedly watching this video footage on the television news each night, I felt a compulsion to be that fireman, to make that kind of difference. Yet I also felt a conflicting disappointment that such opportunities are rarely, if ever, afforded to a lowly security guard like me.

And now here I was confronted with my mug shot plastered all over the newspaper, but not to mark myself as a hero with a red cape across my shoulders—but as the owner of the amazing dog who had averted possible complications from an ensuing bank robbery.

Baby Sweet Cheeks instantly became a public icon. She was invited to parade around the Elk's next monthly meeting, made an appearance at the start of the band concert on St. Patrick's Day, and took center stage at the Malto Animal Shelter's Annual Pet Adoption event. But I must say that despite all the extra attention, Baby didn't let it go to her head and continued to

130

remain forever more a big, sweet and lovable puppy.

"Hey, Justin," Louie said to me a little sheepishly a few days later. "Ah, the people here at Provincial Gardens all pitched in for a collection and they wanted to give Baby Sweet Cheeks a little gift for helping to capture those bank robbers."

On behalf of Baby Sweet Cheeks, I accepted a large cardboard box wrapped with a big red ribbon. Once unwrapped, I uncovered a large, soft doggie bed. I took it out of the box and held it up for Baby to see it for herself. "Well, would you look at this!" I said. "A bed that's finally big enough for all of you!" I set it on the floor and Baby walked over, sniffed it, circled around a couple of times, and comfortably lay down.

"Aww, look at that," Louie said. "And, Justin, we want to take back that former comment . . . you know, the one in which I said she was ugly and needed to leave the complex."

"Baby can stay?"

"Yes, yes, by all means. It'd be our pleasure to have her live here at Provincial Gardens for as long as she likes. She could even be considered our apartment complex mascot if she'd like. Furthermore, if there's anything else we can do to show her our appreciation, just let me know."

"Thanks, Louie," I said. "Letting her stay here is reward enough."

EVER AFTER

Just at the point I had become pretty smug and sure of my relationship with Brenda, I started falling apart at the seams when I realized next month we will have been together for one full year.

Anniversaries, along with other impossible-to-remember special dates, had a way of fogging up and shutting down my basic brain functioning. I had to resort to finding other ways of keeping track of such occasions. The practice of tying little pieces of string around my index finger was becoming too cumbersome, plus it interfered with eating my favorite finger foods, like barbeque spare ribs and sweet corn on the cob, so I reluctantly kept an emergency calendar in the glove compartment of my Volkswagen Beatle.

But I knew circling the date of our anniversary wasn't going to be good enough. I

133

had to formulate a plan of action. I had to do something special for my sweet Brenda. As she already had the perfect security alarm system, namely a Pitty Bull Pinscher, I realized I had to start thinking out of the box for something even more awesome.

And, gulp, I also had to re-evaluate the direction that our relationship was going. I had an idea what the next stage entailed; I just didn't know if I had the courage to take that step. Each day I felt under more and more pressure to do something.

My touchy stomach did the jigger-bug, I developed a tight knot between my shoulder blades, and I tossed and turned in bed so much it felt like I was living inside a revolving hotel doorway.

"Justin, are you o.k?" Brenda would ask.

"Huh? Yeah, sure."

"Are you sure, you're sure? You don't sound so sure."

"Oh, yeah, sure, I'm sure."

My plan of action was to plan a surprise party. I knew Brenda would go all crazy happy if I did, so whenever I found myself in the waiting room of my dentist, or the oil change place, etc., I would carefully search magazines for party ideas that I'd discretely tear from the magazine binding and slip them into my inside jacket pocket. So far I had accumulated a recipe for sprinkle-topped cupcakes, an on-line supplier of large foil-type balloons, and a 10% off coupon for a carpeting steam cleaner. Yikes. That wasn't going to be enough.

I trudged myself downstairs to have a little heart-to-heart with Louie who was in the midst of planning his wedding. Surely he could impart some words of wisdom to party novices like myself.

"Why not book a room at the Malto Taj Mahal on Grand Avenue?" Louie said without taking his eyes from the dandelion-removing tool

135

he was deftly using to dig into the hard impacted clay-and-rocky soil in the front yard of the apartment complex. No apartment manager ever worked more industrious than Louie. If he wasn't pulling weeds, he was hand polishing woodwork, standing on a tall ladder to change hallway ceiling light bulbs, or sweeping leaves off the back parking lot. Louie was an inspiration to our aging and crumbling neighborhood.

"Louie," I said. "We're talking about me here, Justin Maximilian, Security Guard Extraordinaire. I don't have that kind of money stashed in my sock drawer."

In exasperation, Louie wielded his dandelion apparatus in my direction and was about to say something when he stopped himself in frustration. "Oh, yeah, sorry. I got carried away."

We had reached an impasse and stood there with our mouths gapping open like venous fly traps. Then Louie's eyes lit up and he said,

"Why not set up Provincial Gardens' party tent in the back parking lot?"

"A party tent?"

"Yeah, come on. Let's go take a look at it."

After two hours of crawling hands and knees in a dungeon full of enough monster-sized dead arachnoids, nasty mouse droppings, and razor-sharp broken mirrors to give me nightmares for the next seven years, we found it. Despite a few minor rips and tears, I admitted this idea was taking shape. This could be done. *I could do this!*

And besides, Louie assured me that the awful musty smell would evaporate once we aired it out.

Feeling emboldened by Louie's help, I further expanded my party-making horizons by bringing more of my personal contacts on board. I started with recruiting help from my good old friend Bill Taylor. Early on Wednesday night we met for a secret clandestine meeting huddled across from each other in a booth at Egads Corner Bar.

"You're going to need some form of entertainment," he said.

"Entertainment? Like what?"

"You'll need to install a dance floor."

The inside of my mouth went dry and I had to quickly reach for a mouth-quenching sip of beer. I not only had been born with two left feet, but they stuck out so far from side to side that I put a whole new spin on the phrase, "tripped myself up." Nothing good could come about with me being on a dance floor. Not even Brenda could save me there.

"And you'll need a D.J."

"What?" I gulped. "I could never afford a D.J."

"Well, it seems you're in luck," Bill said, smiling. "You're looking at one."

I got so excited that I almost erupted out of character to start dancing with Bill right then and there. But not wanting to kill my newly-discovered bargain D.J., I stopped myself. There would be plenty of time to do that at the party.

My next inspiration took me back to Bart Bartholomew's Car Crushing Show because I had a special favor to ask. "Can I borrow your Chinese lanterns?" I asked. Brenda had always admired Bart's fine art of outdoor lighting and I figured those lanterns would give our party just the right ambiance.

Not one to act in haste, Bart stood there looking above his gravel parking lot. I astutely noticed the tangled mess of electrical cords hanging fifteen feet above us, but I stood my ground until Bart gave up and agreed he'd install them inside the party tent.

"I've got a bunch of chairs and conferences tables I can bring along too," he offered.

"That's great!" I said. "Bring 'em on!"

One thing was leading to another and all my party plans started falling into place. In my excitement, I had to fight to keep myself from smiling and humming when I was hanging out with Brenda. As far as I was concerned, she was a human radar-detection machine. In order to keep my plan a secret for the next two weeks would be a feat unto itself.

Like the petty thieves and hardened criminals whose habits I know so well, I began honing sneaky ways. I hid party favors in Brenda's cardboard hatbox collection, I went online late at night when Brenda was fast asleep to keep track of the attendee's acknowledgements, and I spent more Saturday mornings with Louie planning the final details.

"Yes," I said to myself, "This can be done!"

To keep my surprise from Brenda, I recruited help from Lisa Granger who, for reasons unknown, seemed to be reluctant to help me.

"Ah, I don't know," she said, "I've got another party to attend later that night."

"I only need you to keep Brenda out of here until 1:30 p.m.," I said in my most convincing tone of voice. "You'd have plenty of time to get to your other party."

"Ahhhh, well, o.k." she said.

SURPRISE, SURPRISE

Malto Area Weather Channel Number 54 was predicting scattered thunder showers, but I wasn't buying into it. Armed with Louie's big party tent and the most euphoric feeling ever, I knew this was going to be Brenda's greatest special day. I did start to unravel a little when Lisa Granger arrived a half hour late to pick up Brenda for a shopping trip to buy little Max his first pair of shoes. That only left two hours for Louie, Bill, and I to finish the last final touches to the party.

With paper streamers highlighting the clear-plastic crystal wine glasses, centerpiece bowls heaping full of crunchy corn curds, Bart's Chinese lanterns, and Bill's selection of 50's music, the room emanated with an air of nostalgia and festivity.

When I gave the signal, everyone crouched between the tables. Then Brenda walked in and we all jumped and yelled, "Congratulations!"

I grinned wide and said "Happy Anniversary, Brenda," but besides her mouth gapping open in surprise, I knew something was wrong. Brenda's left eyebrow, along with the rest of that side of her face, drooped in puzzlement and disbelief. My emotions spiraled out of whack and I got that same horrible feeling like in second grade when I forgot to latch the door to the crate belonging to Dennis, our class gerbil. But here I was surrounded with friends and family and I had no idea what I could have done wrong.

Then a few minutes later Brenda recovered, laughed, and threw her arms around me and said, "Oh, Justin! This is so great!"

I blocked her moment of hesitation from my mind and grabbed a hold of Brenda's arm to escort her to the beautifully-decorated chocolate sheet cake from the grocers. Nestled on top of the whipped cream frosting was a laminated super-sized, two-foot-high greeting card. Like I had practiced several times before, I reached over to press its interior activation button. We listened to the King singing, 'Love Me Tender, Love Me True.'

Then the music stopped and Bill spoke into the microphone to announce it was time for our solo dance. A big bull frog jumped into my throat, but I proceeded to ignore him, wrapped my arms around Brenda, closed my eyes, and followed Brenda's led. As it turned out, we didn't do so badly after all. I only stepped on her shoes twice. I figure the second time was cancelled out because of the time she stepped on mine.

Not until everyone was in line for a buffet-style picnic dinner of beans, wieners, and traditional-style potato salad, did I notice the wind was causing the canvass roof of the tent to flap up and down. The more I stared, the more I realized the one little tear above me was beginning to get wider and bigger and . . .

"WATCH OUT!" I screamed as part of the roof caved in on top of us. Claustrophia and panic set in as we became surrounded by a section of foul-smelling canvass, sending me back to memories of being mugged.

I initially threw myself on top of Brenda to protect her. Once I knew she wasn't hurt, I urged her to start crawling until both of us were able to escape underneath the outer edge of the tent. Upon standing again, we watched in horror as our party became a sea of party-goers running in every imaginable direction to avoid the rain and wind. That's when Brenda cupped her hands around her mouth in order to be heard and yelled, "Let's go to Malto Taj Mahal."

Dumbfounded and speechless as to why we'd go there, I followed Brenda as she paved the way with me in tow and five blocks later we walked into the front door of our town's one and only banquet hall. We entered the spacious front hallway furnished with three humongous chandeliers and then we proceeded to Banquet Room No. 1 where I saw the most beautiful decorations and a huge sign which read, "Happy Anniversary, Justin."

Brenda stood there laughing as she watched and waited for everything to register inside my sluggish brain. "You planned a party for me?" I said at last.

"Yep," she said. "Happy Anniversary to you, Justin."

Brenda and I spent the rest of the evening at the most sophisticated and well-planned anniversary party with all our friends. We dined on appetizers of tiny chicken drumsticks and egg rolls, followed by a family-style meal with roast beef and mashed potatoes, mostaccioli and meatballs, and shrimp linguini. And, as rumor has it, I was even seen dancing my head off. I don't know how she did it, but Brenda surpassed my party attempt ten-fold and I knew from that day forward she'd be the one in charge of all our special events.

Tipsy from drinking too much wine, that night we walked hand-in-hand back to Provincial Gardens and stepped inside Brenda's apartment. I wrapped my arms around her, looked into her soft dreamy eyes, and said, "I love you, Brenda. What do you say? Do you want to move in together?"

And beaming with her eyes twinkling like the lights on a Christmas tree, Brenda said, "yes."

Imagine that!

Brenda was going to live with me, Justin Maximilian, Security Guard Extraordinaire.

Kate E. Sebastian, who leads a busy double life by splitting her time between her hometown of Naperville, Illinois, and her vacation home in the northwoods of Wisconsin, says that writing the book "Justin Maximilian, Security Guard Extraordinaire," started as a simple writing exercise. "But once I got started, I felt like I knew Justin and had to keep going so I could share his story with everyone else."

Hopefully this book will help to inspire Kate to complete her other soon-to-be-released novels, including "Driving Under the Radar," about five older women who drive over something in the middle of a storm while on their camping/shopping trip to Mall of America, "Good as Dead," about a serial killer obsessed with killing anyone and everyone who has ever done him wrong, and "The Snitch in DuPage County," about an abused homeless woman who comes to live in a basement apartment beneath a group of ruthless gangbangers.

To keep tabs on Kate Sebastian and her writing progress, check each week on her blog, katesebastianbooks.blogspot.com.